The Perfect Egg Cookbook

Your Ultimate Egg Recipes!

By: Samantha Rich

License Notes

The material presented in this book is the sole intellectual property of the author and is safeguarded by copyright laws. Without written permission from the author, it is strictly prohibited to copy, publish, or distribute any portion or all of the content.

The author has taken great care to ensure the accuracy of the information provided, making it a valuable educational resource. It is the responsibility of the reader to handle the book with care, as the author will not be held responsible for any misuse or resulting consequences.

Table of Contents

Introduction 6

The importance of eggs in your diet 7

  1. Haystack Eggs 8

  2. Strawberry Egg Muffins 10

  3. Chocolate Chip Oatmeal 12

  4. Blueberry Lemon Microwave Muffin 14

  5. Fried Spaghetti Frittata 16

  6. Beef Omelet 18

  7. Green Onion & Cream Cheese Scrambled Eggs 20

  8. Peanut Butter Chocolate Muffins 22

  9. Chicken Omurice 24

  10. Chopped California Cobb Salad 26

  11. Egg on Tomato Pizza 28

  12. Ham Filled Microwave Omelet 31

  13. Creamy Scalloped Eggs 33

  14. Dark Chocolate Egg Pudding 35

  15. Hot and Sour Egg Soup 37

  16. Egg Lemon Soup 39

17. Eggs Florentine...41

18. Anchovy-Egg Boats...44

19. Spicy and Eggy Crumpets..46

20. Porky Crepe Roll..48

21. Crispy Egg Tempuras..50

22. Spam and Eggs in Crisp Seaweed Wrap...52

23. Eggy Pesto Melt...54

24. Gooey Egg n' Chocolate Dessert..56

25. Classic Egg Pudding...58

26. Egg and Lime Dessert...60

27. Sunny-Side-Up egg Muffins..62

28. Spicy and Scrumptious Muffins...64

29. Golden Egg Curry..66

30. Eggs in Red Curry..68

31. Basic Italian Omelet...70

32. Cream Cheese Omelet with Herbs..72

33. Mushroom Quiche..74

34. A Hearty Australian Omelet..76

35. Oats & Blueberry Cake...78

36. Dandelion Olives Quiche..80

37. Onions & Swiss Chard Quiche.. 82

38. Eggs in Purgatory 84

39. Tomato Quiche 86

40. Frittata with Asparagus and Tomato.. 88

41. Prosciutto Eggs 90

42. Egg Cooker Whoopie Pie... 92

43. Buttery Eggs 94

44. Pepperoni Omelet 96

45. Bacon Omelet... 98

46. Spicy Deviled Eggs... 100

47. Macaroni and Eggs 102

48. Red Beet Deviled Eggs 104

49. Avocado Herb Deviled Eggs 106

50. Eggs in Bread 108

51. Soy Sriracha Deviled Eggs... 110

52. Tomato, Basil Mozzarella Quiche 112

Conclusion 114

Biography 115

Afterword's.. 116

Introduction

Are you an avid egg consumer who adores eating eggs for breakfast, lunch, or supper? You must be aware at this point that these meals are the most significant of the day. Therefore, it's crucial for our general health to have at least an egg meal. Contrary to common assumptions, cooking most meals doesn't have to be a pain, especially if you have an egg cooker. Egg cookers come in a range of sizes and shapes, from little electric models that you can just plug in and let to work to bigger ones that you can just take out and let do their job.

We will look at some amazing, fast, and delectable meal ideas in our ultimate egg cookbook. The best part is that these dishes don't have to be consumed only for lunch, dinner, or brunch. You are free to make breakfast foods for supper in your home if it is something you enjoy doing. Enjoy these recipes on your own, or impress your loved ones by whipping up delectable meals in no time. We're about to take use of all the possibilities that exist.

The importance of eggs in your diet

Even the most challenging pastries seem more achievable if you know more about the many components of an egg, such as the whites, yolks, and so on, and how to treat them. The behavior and functioning of eggs in these recipes can significantly impact the final product of your meal or recipe. Cakes, desserts, meringues, and pastry cream are baked delicacies that rely heavily on eggs. They offer batters stability and strength, thicken and emulsion sauces and custards, moisten cakes and other baked products, and can even be used as glue or frosting.

In recipes that call for the yolk, the fat content and emulsifying abilities of the egg yolk are extensively employed. The fat gives prepared dishes a deeper flavor and smoother texture. Another of the yolk's extraordinary qualities is its unique ability to blend fats and liquids into an emulsion that prevents them from separating.

1. Haystack Eggs

It's simple to miss breakfast and have a bad start to the day, but with these delicious breakfast haystacks, you'll want to schedule time to eat. You may make this meal for breakfast every morning throughout the workweek. On the other hand, if it's the weekend or a holiday, you might want to try something a bit more unique to eat with the haystack eggs.

Serving Size: 4

Cooking Time: 13 Minutes

Ingredients:

- 1 cup cheddar cheese, shredded
- 6 bacon slices, cooked and crumbled
- 1 tbsp. fresh parsley, finely chopped
- 1 ½ oz. can shoestring potatoes
- 4 eggs

Instructions:

a) Have your oven preheated to 350°F; spray your baking pan (8" square) with nonstick cooking spray. Spread the shoestring potatoes in the bottom of the baking pan. Make 4 indentations in the potatoes with the back of a spoon large enough for the eggs.

b) Break an egg into each indentation. Bake for 8 minutes. Sprinkle the cheddar, cheese, bacon and parsley over the eggs.

c) Bake for 5 minutes or until the eggs are set.

d) Remove the pan from the oven and serve. You can substitute fried shoestring French-fried potatoes if desired.

2. Strawberry Egg Muffins

This wonderful fruit muffin serves as a delectable morning side dish. Use up your spring and summer strawberries by making strawberry muffins. They taste just as good and offer a great twist from the typical blueberry muffin. The key to a healthy diet is including an egg yolk in the cooking process. Additionally, doing so gives the muffins a very rich flavor.

Serving Size: 1

Cooking Time: 1 Minute

Ingredients:

- 2 tbsps. sugar
- 1 egg yolk
- 3 tbsps. strawberries, diced
- 3 tbsps. flour
- 1 tbsp. milk

Instructions:

a) Combine egg yolk, milk, flour and strawberries and stir well.

b) Add the remaining ingredients, fold to combine, and set to microwave on high, without the cover, until cooked through for about 1 minute and 15 seconds.

c) Serve, and enjoy.

3. Chocolate Chip Oatmeal

To your oatmeal for breakfast, mix in a few chocolate chips. The ideal blend of ingredients, including egg yolk, is present in these delectable oatmeal chocolate chip cookies. On the inside, they are great because they are soft and chewy. It takes the perfect amount of salt to balance out the powerful flavors of chocolate and walnuts.

Serving Size: 1

Cooking Time: 5 Minutes

Ingredients:

- ⅛ tsp. salt
- ½ cup chocolate chips
- 1 egg
- ½ cup oats, quick
- 1 tbsp. walnuts, chopped
- ½ cup milk

Instructions:

a) Combine all your ingredients, except almonds, in your Ceramic Egg Cooker, stir well, and set in your microwave to cook, without the cover for about a minute.

b) Remove and stir, then return to microwave to cook until your oatmeal has been fully cooked through, stirring in 10 second intervals.

c) Top with walnuts, and more chocolate chips.

d) Serve, and enjoy.

4. Blueberry Lemon Microwave Muffin

This mouthwatering bread muffin is the ideal side for breakfast. Fresh blueberries are used in these straightforward muffins. This dish is fantastic for lazy summer nights when you want a sweet treat! It is a straightforward, fluffy, and moist muffin that can be made quickly and with minimal mess. It is one of the greatest because of the large, luscious blueberries, tart lemon, and egg yolk.

Serving Size: 1

Cooking Time: 1 Minute

Ingredients:

- ¼ tsp. baking powder
- 2 tbsps. blueberries, frozen
- 1 egg, yolk
- 1 tsp. lemon zest
- 1 tbsp. butter, melted
- ½ tsp. vanilla
- 3 tbsps. flour
- 2 tbsps. sugar
- 1 tbsp. milk

Instructions:

a) Combine your butter, egg, milk and vanilla and stir well.

b) Add the remaining ingredients, fold to combine, and set to microwave on high, without the cover, until cooked through for about 1 minute and 15 seconds.

c) Serve, and enjoy.

5. Fried Spaghetti Frittata

Using leftover spaghetti, you may create this tasty new dish in a unique way. You may make your omelet by combining it with eggs that are creamy. Make this fantastic fried spaghetti frittata with your leftovers! The dish is healthy for your family and really simple to modify.

Serving Size: 3

Cooking Time: 6 Minutes

Ingredients:

- 1 tbsp. chopped parsley
- 1 medium sized onion, chopped
- ¼ cup milk
- 2 cups cooked spaghetti
- 1 tbsp. grated cheddar cheese
- Salt and pepper to taste
- 1 tbsp. grated parmesan cheese
- 4 large eggs

Instructions:

a) In a sizable mixing bowl, beat the eggs, milk, parsley, cheese, onion, salt and pepper. Add in the cooked spaghetti.

b) In a nonstick skillet, over medium heat, pour in the egg mixture. Cook for 6 minutes.

c) Use an inverted plate to flip the frittata. Cook the other side again for about six minutes or until golden.

6. Beef Omelet

Your entire family will love the tasty omelet that this recipe makes. It is distinctive in that the omelet is prepared more like a pancake and contains pieces of beef and eggs, which are the main components. It makes a delectable meal for breakfast, a quick lunch, or a snack.

Serving Size: 2

Cooking Time: 1 Minute

Ingredients:

- 2 tbsps. onions, chopped
- 2 tbsps. milk
- ⅛ tsp. salt
- 2 deli beef slices, chopped
- 2 eggs
- 1 tbsp. Brie cheese

Instructions:

a) Combine the eggs, milk and salt in your Ceramic Egg Cooker. Cover then rest your finger on top of the small hole in the lid and shake well to combine. Stir in your chopped deli meat and cheese.

b) Set to cook in the microwave, covered, for about a minute on high.

c) Remove and stir, then return to cook until fully cooked through, stirring in 20-second intervals.

d) Serve, and enjoy.

7. Green Onion & Cream Cheese Scrambled Eggs

The best scrambled eggs are made up of cream cheese and green onion. The few recipe ingredients contribute to this meal's sweetness with cream cheese playing a better part. It is a recipe y

Serving Size: 3

Cooking Time: 10 Minutes

Ingredients:

- 4 green onions, chopped
- 3 tbsps. unsalted butter
- 6 eggs
- 3 oz. cream cheese, cubed
- ¼ tsp. salt
- ½ cup whole milk
- 1/8 tsp. black pepper

Instructions:

a) Bring the eggs, milk, cream cheese, salt and black pepper to a blender. Process until smooth and combined. Turn the blender off and stir in the green onions.

b) Place your butter in a skillet over medium heat to melt. Add the eggs. Do not stir until the eggs begin to set on the bottom. Stir frequently and cook until set, but moist.

c) Have the skillet from the fire and serve.

8. Peanut Butter Chocolate Muffins

This gooey, peanut buttery muffin is a fantastic snack for youngsters. A straightforward recipe for soft, moist peanut butter muffins. There is no need for a mixer while making these muffins. Don't skip the egg yolk.

Serving Size: 1

Cooking Time: 1 Minute

Ingredients:

- ¼ tsp. baking powder
- 2 tbsps. hot chocolate, power
- 1 egg yolk
- ½ tsp. vanilla extract
- 3 tbsps. flour
- 1 tbsp. milk
- 2 tbsps. sugar
- 1 tbsp. butter
- 1 tsp. peanut butter

Instructions:

a) Combine vanilla extract, butter, egg yolk and milk and stir well.

b) Add the remaining ingredients, fold to combine, and set to microwave on high, without the cover, until cooked through for about 1 minute and 15 seconds.

c) Serve, and enjoy.

9. Chicken Omurice

This omelet recipe is unique from others. Every dinner night will be memorable thanks to a mainstay of modern Japanese cuisine created with savory chicken fried rice wrapped in a thick and silky omelet. This is one of those recipes that both children and adults enjoy since it has sweet and savory chicken and rice on the inside, and you may decorate the top with whatever you wish.

Serving Size: 1

Cooking Time: 10 Minutes

Ingredients:

- 1 ½ tbsps. tomato ketchup
- 2 tbsps. diced carrots
- ½ tbsp. diced onion
- ½ cup cooked rice
- 2 eggs
- 1/8 teaspoon salt and pepper
- ½ tsp. olive oil
- 2 tbsps. heavy cream
- 1 tsp. minced garlic
- ½ cup shredded cooked chicken

Instructions:

a) Make the omelet by whisking the cream, eggs and salt in a bowl.

b) Heat oil into a nonstick pan over medium heat. Cook until the carrots are tender and the onions are translucent after adding the onions, carrots, and garlic.

c) Add the chicken and rice. Then add the ketchup. Cook until the mixture is warmed up. Season with salt and pepper. Take out of the pan and set aside.

d) In the same pan, pour the egg mixture stirring gently to form curds. Turn the pan to low and cover it with the lid.

e) The eggs are done when they are already thickened and aren't runny anymore. At this point, get the rice and spoon it on the half side of the egg, making sure to leave a border at the edge of the egg.

f) Fold the egg and seal the edges.

g) Serve.

10. Chopped California Cobb Salad

You may serve this delectable salad for lunch or dinner. For a great dinner or lunch the following day, try this fresh Cobb salad that is filled with cheese, turkey bacon, chicken, and eggs. A fantastic way to eat healthily while using up leftover chicken or turkey!

Serving Size: 6

Cooking Time: 2 ½ Minutes

Ingredients:

- 1 cup grape tomatoes
- 2 romaine Lettuce heads, washed, dried and shredded
- ½ cup blue cheese, crumbled
- 1 lb. tender chicken, grilled and chopped
- 2 eggs
- 3 turkey bacon slices, crispy and diced

Dressing

- 1 tbsp. bell pepper herb rub
- ¼ tsp. salt
- ½ cup Greek yogurt
- 3 tbsps. milk
- 1 avocado, ripe
- 1 tbsp. lemon juice

Instructions:

a) Add an egg and top with ½ cup of water in each cup of your egg cooker.

b) Lightly pierce the yolk of the egg with a fork. Set the eggs to cook along with other ingredients except for the dressing ones, on high, until the eggs have become hard cooked for about 2½ minutes.

c) Remove cooked egg from water, allow to cool slightly, and roughly chop. Add all your dressing ingredients in a food processor and pulse until fully combined, and smooth.

d) Spread your dressing in a salad bowl, top with salad, toss and serve.

11. Egg on Tomato Pizza

This one is for all pizza lovers. Get to start your day with your favorite comfort meal. Make this comfortable thin-crust pizza by combining a high-quality, thick tomato sauce with the ideal eggs, which should have golden yolks and a creamy texture.

Serving Size: 3

Cooking Time: 12 Minutes

Ingredients:

For the dough:

- 5 oz. bread flour
- ½ tsp. salt
- 2 ½ tsps. olive oil
- ½ cup water
- ¾ tsp. instant dry yeast
- Cornmeal for dusting

For the toppings and sauce:

- 4 cloves garlic
- 2 tbsps. olive oil
- 4 tbsps. tomato sauce
- 1 ½ tsp. dried basil
- 1 cup grated mozzarella cheese
- 3 large eggs

Instructions:

a) Sprinkle the yeast over some warm water and let sit for 15 minutes or until bubbly and yeast has activated.

b) Add the olive oil, salt and add ¼ cup and 2 teaspoons of bread flour. Stir with a wooden spoon to form sticky dough.

c) Put the remaining flour on a surface then transfer the dough. Knead for about ten minutes.

d) Transfer into a bowl greased with olive oil. Cover with plastic wrap and place it somewhere warm for about 1 hour to help it rise and double in volume.

e) Meanwhile, preheat your oven to 4500F.

f) Dust the baking sheet with cornmeal. Transfer the dough into the baking sheet then punch down to remove the air. Press to desired shape. Let rest for 15 more minutes.

g) To make the sauce: In a skillet over medium heat, warm some olive oil then sauté the garlic. Add the tomato sauce and dried basil.

h) Spoon the sauce on top of the pizza dough, sprinkle evenly with the mozzarella then top with 3 eggs.

i) Bake for about 12 minutes until the crust is golden. Serve.

12. Ham Filled Microwave Omelet

Since breakfast is the most significant meal of the day, prepare an omelet in your microwave that is high in protein and deliciously cheesy. The Ham Filled Microwave Omelet, which includes green onions, ham, cheese, and eggs, is a dish on another level. A meal has never been this quick to prepare—just a few minutes!

Serving Size: 2

Cooking Time: 1 Minute

Ingredients:

- 1/8 cup ham, chopped
- 1 tbsp. cheddar cheese
- 2 eggs
- Salt
- 2 tbsps. milk
- 2 tbsps. green onions, chopped

Instructions:

a) Combine the eggs, milk and salt in your Ceramic Egg Cooker. Cover, rest your finger on top of the small hole in the lid and shake well to combine. Stir in your ham and cheese.

b) Set to cook in the microwave, covered, for about a minute on high.

c) Remove and stir, then return to cook until fully cooked through, stirring in 20-second intervals.

d) Serve, and enjoy.

13. Creamy Scalloped Eggs

An egg casserole dish with salted bacon, hard-boiled eggs, and other delicious ingredients. It tastes fantastic for a lavish meal as well as for breakfast. It could be your favorite dish—cheesy, creamy, and always excellent.

Serving Size: 2

Cooking Time: 30 Minutes

Ingredients:

- 5 sliced bacon, fried until crispy then crumbles into small bits
- ¼ cup panko bread crumbs
- ¼ cup parmesan cheese
- 3 hard-boiled eggs, sliced
- ¾ tbsp. butter
- 4 tbsps. grated cheddar cheese
- 2 tbsps. finely sliced onions
- 1 tbsp. flour
- 1 cup milk

Instructions:

a) In a skillet over medium heat, melt some butter then sauté the onions until it is translucent. Make a roux by adding the flour, and cook for a few seconds to remove the raw floury taste. Then add the milk, cheese and cook until the sauce has thickened and cheese has melted. Set aside

b) In a baking dish, layer the egg slices, then pour over the sauce, then sprinkle with mixed parmesan and breadcrumbs.

c) Bake for about 30 minutes until the top is golden brown in color. Cool for a bit before serving.

14. Dark Chocolate Egg Pudding

Make your experience eating egg pudding even more memorable. Make this decadent, creamy chocolate pudding for yourself. It has hard yet tender borders and a jiggly center that oozes warm, smooth, and silky liquid chocolate custard.

Serving Size: 6

Cooking Time: 10 Minutes

Ingredients:

- 1 tbsp. sweetened cocoa powder
- 1/3 cup self-rising flour
- ¼ cup butter
- 3 eggs
- ½ cup dark chocolate, chopped
- 1/3 cup all-purpose flour
- ½ cup brown sugar

Instructions:

a) Preheat your oven to 3500F.

b) Grease 6 pudding molds.

c) Melt butter and chocolate in a saucepan, about 3 minutes.

d) Beat the eggs and sugar until pale in color. Fold in flour, cocoa and chocolate mixture.

e) Pour mixture into prepared molds. Bake for 10 minutes until the edges are firm.

f) Serve and enjoy.

15. Hot and Sour Egg Soup

A nutritious soup that is fast, light, elegant, and soothing. With the help of eggs, bamboo shoots, and mushrooms, this savory soup is smooth. This makes a filling supper when paired with some crusty bread. It's easy to customize to your individual taste preferences, fast, and simple to prepare.

Serving Size: 2

Cooking Time: 5 Minutes

Ingredients:

- 2 beaten eggs
- 2 tbsps. rice wine vinegar
- 1/8 tsp. pepper
- 14 oz. chicken broth
- ½ cup thinly sliced carrots
- 2 tbsps. water
- ¼ cup sliced mushrooms
- 4 oz. bamboo shoots, drained
- ½ tbsp. soy sauce
- 1 tbsp. cornstarch
- ½ cup green peas

Instructions:

a) In a sizable saucepan over medium heat, combine peas, carrots, bamboo shoots mushrooms, soy sauce and vinegar. Let it boil then lower down the heat and continue to simmer for 5 minutes.

b) In a sizable bowl, mix water and cornstarch until it dissolves. Pour it slowly into the soup and mix to incorporate.

c) Gently pour in the eggs and mix. Turn off the heat and serve.

16. Egg Lemon Soup

A delicious rice soup that is lightened by the tangy flavor of lemons and made creamier, thicker, and creamier by eggs. Make it a complete supper by adding some shredded meat for further nutrients.

Serving Size: 2

Cooking Time: 20 Minutes

Ingredients:

- 1 egg
- 2 cups chicken stock
- Salt and pepper to taste
- 1 ½ tbsps. lemon juice
- 2 tbsps. uncooked rice

Instructions:

a) In a sizeable saucepan over medium heat, bring the stock to a boil. Add the uncooked rice and cook for 20 minutes until tender, stirring occasionally so that it does not stick.

b) Reduce the heat down to low the simmer.

c) In a sizable bowl, whisk together the lemon juice and eggs until smooth.

d) Temper the eggs by ladling ½ cup broth into the egg mixture, whisk until combined.

e) Pour in the egg mixture back into the pan, then cook until the soup has thickened. Serve.

17. Eggs Florentine

With a twist, the typical poached eggs with rich hollandaise sauce, plentiful slices of ham, and wonderfully toasted English muffins will give you a remarkable experience. Making your typical breakfast more fun and nutritious by including spinach can help you start the day off on the right foot. By including any of your preferred vegetables, feel free to be inventive and create your own version.

Serving Size: 2

Cooking Time: 3 Minutes

Ingredients:

- 1 English muffin, split
- 2 slices ham
- 1 tsp. white vinegar
- ½ tbsp. unsalted butter
- 1 bunch baby spinach
- 2 large eggs

For the hollandaise sauce:

- 2 tbsps. and 2 tsps. unsalted butter, melted
- Salt and pepper to taste
- 1 egg yolk
- ¾ tsp. lemon juice

Instructions:

a) Over low heat, bring half a saucepan's worth of water to a simmer.

b) In a bowl, whisk together the egg yolk and lemon juice, until it reaches a light pale color.

c) Fit the bowl on top of the saucepan and continue whisking. Then while still whisking, pour the butter in a steady, slow stream and whisk until the sauce thickens. Season with salt and pepper. Set aside.

d) To start poaching the eggs, fill a large saucepan with water, add the vinegar and bring to a gentle boil.

e) Break each egg and drop it in the saucepan carefully. Cook for 3 minutes in a slow boil.

f) While poaching the eggs, split the English muffin in half and spread some butter on the cut side generously.

g) On another skillet, toast the muffins cut side down. Set aside. In the same skillet, cook the ham.

h) When the eggs are cooked, use a slotted spoon to get it out of the saucepan and use a paper towel to absorb excess water.

i) Lastly, blanch the baby spinach.

j) To assemble, place the muffins and put some spinach over the top, then the ham, and then the poached eggs. Finish it off with the hollandaise sauce you made earlier.

18. Anchovy-Egg Boats

Here, you get a pleasant encounter with aggressive anchovies thanks to the rich hard-boiled eggs and a liberal drizzle of olive oil. This is delicious, served with drinks as well as in the morning, when it is sliced into little pieces. Best quality anchovies in a creamy, salty egg salad served in crisp lettuce boats. For the ideal starter, drizzle with a special dressing and sprinkle some croutons on top.

Serving Size: 3

Cooking Time: 5 Minutes

Ingredients:

- 2 tbsps. anchovy fillets, stripped
- ¼ cup store bought croutons
- 3 pieces hard boiled eggs
- ½ tbsp. olive oil
- 1 gem lettuce

For the dressing:

- ½ cup extra virgin olive oil
- 1 egg yolk
- 1 tbsp. lemon juice
- ¼ tsp. sugar
- 1 ½ tsps. mustard
- Salt and pepper to taste
- 1 tsp. crushed garlic

Instructions:

a) In a bowl, mix all ingredients together for the dressing except the olive oil. Then pour the oil in a slow steady stream while whisking, to produce a smooth dressing.

b) Shell the hard-boiled eggs and slice into squares.

c) Arrange 2 pieces of lettuce in a serving platter, add the boiled eggs then top with croutons and sprinkle with dressing.

d) Serve and enjoy.

19. Spicy and Eggy Crumpets

These savory crumpets, which are subsequently cooked till exquisitely golden brown, may provide a particular touch to any meal. Crispy bacon and sweet maple syrup are a wonderful addition to this amazing and extremely delicious recipe.

Serving Size: 1

Cooking Time: 5 Minutes

Ingredients:

- 2 slices smoked bacon
- 1/8 tsp. minced red chili
- Maple syrup, as desired
- Salt and pepper to taste
- 1 tsp. olive oil
- 2 round crumpets
- 1 large egg

Instructions:

a) In a bowl, whisk the egg and season with salt and pepper, and then add in the minced chili.

b) In a nonstick pan over medium heat, warm some olive oil then fry the bacon until crispy. Set aside.

c) Get the crumpets and dip them into the egg and chili mixture, then fry for a few minutes until golden. Flip and cook until the sides are also golden.

d) Top with the slices of bacon then drizzle with maple syrup.

e) Serve and enjoy.

20. Porky Crepe Roll

Think of them as crepes with eggs on top and a pork filling inside. To make a crepe-thin egg omelet, a generous amount of light and fluffy dry pig meat is folded up. With this recipe, you may have a delicious, lighter version of a hearty, complete omelet.

Serving Size: 2

Cooking Time: 2 Minutes

Ingredients:

- Salt and pepper to taste
- 1 tbsp. chopped chives
- 2 tbsps. mayonnaise
- 2 eggs
- ½ cup pork floss

Instructions:

a) Whisk together the eggs, chives, salt and pepper. Mix until well combined.

b) In a large, non-stick skillet, in medium heat, pour in the mixture and swirl around to coat the whole pan and to make a thin omelet. Cook for around 2 minutes or until the eggs have set.

c) Remove from the pan and put the omelet on a plate.

d) To assemble, brush some mayonnaise on the omelet then sprinkle it with the pork floss. Roll it up and cut it into 1-inch slices.

21. Crispy Egg Tempuras

Give your normal egg dishes a little crunch. Apply some breadcrumbs to them, then cook them in hot oil until crispy and brown. Crunchy exterior and soft, runny yolks within make a delicious combination.

Serving Size: 2

Cooking Time: 7 Minutes

Ingredients:

- 2 eggs
- 1 egg, beaten
- 3 cups vegetable oil
- 2 tbsps. flour
- Salt and pepper to taste
- 2 tbsps. panko breadcrumbs mixed together with 1 tablespoon grated parmesan

Instructions:

a) In a medium saucepan, bring the water into a boil then carefully drop the eggs into the boiling water. Make sure the eggs are fully covered by the water. Cook for 6 minutes. Lift the eggs using a slotted spoon then immediately rinse the cooked eggs into running water.

b) Peel off the egg shells when the eggs are completely cool. Set aside.

c) Place the flour, the eggs, and then the breadcrumb parmesan mixture into 3 separate plates. Coat the eggs with flour first, then dip in egg mixture then coat with the breadcrumb and parmesan mixture

d) Heat the vegetable in a frying pan, over medium high heat. Using a slotted spoon, begin deep frying the eggs one at a time for around 30 seconds until the oil begins to sizzle. You'll know when they're done when the breadcrumbs are crispy and golden brown in color. Drain in paper towels to remove excess oil.

e) Season with salt and pepper before serving.

22. Spam and Eggs in Crisp Seaweed Wrap

With molded sticky rice, a properly cooked egg, and a layer of spam marinated in a unique sweet-soy sauce, this robust and delicious meal is completely wrapped in salty, crisp seaweed sheets. Grab a wrap for your entire lunch or dinner.

Serving Size: 5

Cooking Time: 3 Minutes

Ingredients:

- 1 tbsp. vegetable oil
- 2 2/3 cups cooked Japanese short grain rice and 3 tbsps. rice vinegar mixture
- 2 tbsps. oyster sauce
- 6 oz. spam
- 3 sheets nori, dry seaweed sheets
- 1 ¾ tbsps. soy sauce
- 4 eggs, beaten
- 3 tbsps. brown sugar

Instructions:

a) In a sizable bowl, stir together the soy sauce, sugar and oyster sauce, and mix until sugar is completely dissolved.

b) Slice the spam into 5 slices then marinate in the prepared sauce for 5 minutes.

c) Heat a nonstick skillet over medium heat, heat some vegetable oil then fry the spam slices until lightly browned.

d) In a nonstick skillet, cook the eggs and spread it evenly into the pan, making it ¼ inch thick. Cut into 5 equal pieces.

e) Cut the seaweed sheets in half and lay them on your work surface.

f) Put the rice press into the center of the nori sheet, the pack rice firmly inside the mold. Top with some egg. Wrap some nori tightly, and then seal the edges with some water.

g) Serve.

23. Eggy Pesto Melt

Thick pieces of bread, rich eggs, and melt-in-your-mouth mozzarella cheese are combined to create a filling sandwich that is both nutritious and wholesome. Make this if you don't have time to prepare dinner.

Serving Size: 1

Cooking Time: 5 Minutes

Ingredients:

- 2 slices bread
- 1 tbsp. pesto sauce
- 1 tsp. olive oil
- ¼ cup mozzarella cheese, shredded
- 1 egg

Instructions:

a) In a sizable bowl, whisk together the egg and pesto until combined.

b) Heat a nonstick pan over medium heat then warm up some olive oil.

c) When the edges are firm, pour the egg mixture into the pan and cook for one minute.

d) Fold the edges of the omelet to make a square shaped omelet to fit the sandwich. Set aside.

e) On the same skillet, put in the bread and half of the cheese and cook until the cheese has melted. Top with the egg and the remaining cheese, then top with the remaining slice of bread. Flip and cook the other side until bread is toasted and all the cheese is melted.

f) Serve.

24. Gooey Egg n' Chocolate Dessert

Not only is this delicious chocolate and egg dish among the tastiest you will ever eat, it is also among the simplest. For a better experience, the gooey treat incorporates all of the preferred ingredients, including salt, eggs, and bittersweet chocolate.

Serving Size: 7

Cooking Time: 10 Minutes

Ingredients:

- 12 tbsps. unsalted butter
- 4 large eggs
- 8 oz. bittersweet chocolate, chopped
- 1/8 tsps. salt
- ½ cup sugar

Instructions:

a) Preheat the oven at 350^0F. Grease 7 ramekins. Use a double boiler to melt chocolate.

b) Meanwhile, whip up the eggs, salt and sugar. When the chocolate has cooled down a bit, mix it in the eggs.

c) Divide the batter equally in the ramekins. Bake in the oven for around 10 minutes or until the sides are done but the centers are gooey.

d) Cool a bit before serving.

25. Classic Egg Pudding

It is hassle-free, straightforward, and absolutely wonderful. This traditional egg pudding is a smooth, sweet dessert that is prepared with a deft blending of sugar, eggs, and milk. It is delicious and healthful to sometimes cook for your family as part of your meal plans.

Serving Size: 6

Cooking Time: 60 Minutes

Ingredients:

- 1 cup sugar
- 3 cups milk
- 6 eggs

Instructions:

a) Preheat the oven at 350^0F. Take a sauce pan and add 3 tablespoons of sugar to it. Let it melt over medium heat. Just as it has completely melted, pour in the base of the pudding dish. Swirl the pudding dish with your hands so that the melted sugar coats the entire bottom and some sides.

b) Beat the eggs and remaining sugar with a beater; add milk and beat well again. Pour mixture over caramel base and bake in the oven in a hot water bath for about an hour.

c) Insert a toothpick to check for doneness.

26. Egg and Lime Dessert

This dish is a must-try because of its light and energizing tastes. Juices with lemon and lime are popular throughout the summer. The preparation of the juices, egg yolks, and other essential components is simple and makes for a wonderful dining experience.

Serving Size: 15

Cooking Time: 4 Minutes

Ingredients:

- ¼ cup lemon juice
- ½ gallon vanilla ice cream softened
- 2 eggs, lightly beaten
- 1 ¼ cup sugar, divided
- 1-quart lime sherbet
- 14 tbsps. butter, divided, melted
- 1 ½ cups graham crackers, crumbed

Instructions:

a) In a mixing bowl, mix together crumbs, ¼ cup sugar and half the butter. Press it into a sizable dish and let it freeze till the base is firm.

b) In another bowl, mix ice cream and lime sherbet and pour over the base; freeze again. Add eggs, lemon juice, remaining sugar and butter to a heavy saucepan and cook on low heat, stirring continuously until mixture coats back of metal spoon. Refrigerate the mixture till cooled.

c) Spread the egg mix over ice cream and freeze for 3 hours. Cut in squares before serving.

27. Sunny-Side-Up egg Muffins

This is a sweet little twist on the typical breakfast muffin. With these simple-to-make muffins, you can have twice the pleasure while making a lot less effort in the kitchen. Preparing sunny-side-up egg muffins has to be among the easiest things you've ever done.

Serving Size: 6

Cooking Time: 35 Minutes

Ingredients:

- ½ cup sliced green onion
- Black pepper to taste
- 12 slices pre-cooked bacon
- Butter for slices
- 1 cup grated cheddar cheese
- 3 slices white bread
- 12 eggs
- Salt as desired

Instructions:

a) Put the oven to 350^0F settings. Butter the slices nicely and then cut into quarters. With the buttered side down, place each quarter into each of the muffin cavities in the standard muffin pan. Crack open one egg over each of the slices. Sprinkle some pepper & salt on top. Cut up the bacon to fit in the muffin holes. After adding bacon, sprinkle cheese and onions on each of the muffins.

b) Place the tray in the oven before baking for 35 minutes. Let them cool for a few minutes outside of the oven so they can be taken out easily.

28. Spicy and Scrumptious Muffins

Nothing beats enjoying delicious, spicy, and mouthwatering muffins when you first wake up. It's impossible for your world to be more pleasant than when you can smell the wonderful aroma throughout your home or kitchen. Use the simple instructions for preparation and treat your family to these delicious muffins.

Serving Size: 7

Cooking Time: 20 Minutes

Ingredients:

- Cooking spray
- ½ cup diced red bell pepper
- ½ cup cheddar cheese, shredded
- 7 eggs
- ¼ cup chopped onion
- 1 clove garlic, chopped
- ½ tsp. cumin
- ½ cup roasted green chilies, drained
- ¼ cup milk
- Salt and pepper to taste
- ¼ cup chopped jalapeno
- 1 tbsp. coconut oil

Instructions:

a) Preheat the oven to 350^0F. Heat oil in medium skillet on medium heat and sauté onion, garlic, jalapeno and pepper. Cook until onions are transparent and pepper has softened. Take off heat and cool.

b) In the meanwhile, take a large bowl and whisk up the eggs with milk. Add salt, pepper, chilies and cumin to the eggs. When the onion mixture has cooled, add it to the eggs and mix again.

c) Grease the muffin tins with coating spray and add egg mixture till the tins are ¾ full.

d) Bake for 20 minutes or until firm and done.

29. Golden Egg Curry

One of the ingredients in the kitchen that is probably used the most is the egg. This kind of preparation will allow you to try them out better. When hosting friends for supper, you might want to include the Golden Egg Curry because it is a really attractive meal.

Serving Size: 6

Cooking Time: 5 Minutes

Ingredients:

- 400ml can coconut cream
- 1 tsp. turmeric
- 2 tomatoes, finely chopped
- 12 curry leaves
- 6 eggs
- 1 thinly sliced onion
- Salt to taste
- 2 tbsps. oil
- 2 tsps. mustard seeds

Instructions:

a) Boil the eggs. Heat the oil in a saucepan and cook the onion till golden.

b) Add mustard seeds, curry leaves, tomato and turmeric. Cook until seeds pop.

c) Add coconut cream and let it simmer for 10 minutes or until gravy is thick. Add the eggs and cook for another minute.

d) Serve with rice.

30. Eggs in Red Curry

Egg in Red Curry is a delightful onion and tomato dish with a deep flavor. These are delicious when made with a mixture of hard-boiled eggs, butter, and lemon juice, among other ingredients. Indians commonly consume this dish, which is extremely representative of the country.

Serving Size: 6

Cooking Time: 5 Minutes

Ingredients:

- 4 tbsps. butter
- 1 tbsp. lemon juice
- Salt and pepper to taste
- 2 tbsps. each curry powder and tomato paste
- 1 clove garlic, crushed
- 2 tbsps. chopped parsley
- Zest of 1 lemon
- 6 eggs, hard boiled and halved
- ¾ cup water
- 1 medium onion, chopped

Instructions:

a) Melt butter and sauté onion and garlic in a pan; cook till onion is tender.

b) Add tomato paste, water, curry powder, salt, pepper and lemon juice. Simmer the mixture until fat starts to appear on the sides.

c) Add eggs and let them heat through.

d) Garnish with zest and parsley before serving.

31. Basic Italian Omelet

Although this omelet isn't entirely Italian, it does contain many characteristics that make it fit to be. For instance, it is fried in olive oil and is done in a hot pan relatively quickly until it turns a wonderful golden-brown color.

Serving Size: 2

Cooking Time: 6 Minutes

Ingredients:

- 2 tbsps. goat cheese, crumbled
- 6 eggs
- 1 tbsp. chopped chives
- ¼ cup olive oil
- Salt and pepper to taste

Instructions:

a) Crumble the goat cheese in a bowl. Cut the chives, beat the eggs in a separate bowl and keep the seasonings handy. Pour the oil in a skillet big enough to hold omelet of 6 eggs and let it heat up over medium heat. Make sure the whole pan is coated.

b) When the pan is heated, pour the beaten eggs. You will notice that the eggs will start to bubble almost right away and will firm up immediately.

c) Help the omelet by lifting its sides. The uncooked egg will run towards the sides. When you notice that the egg is not runny anymore, yet slightly undercooked then it is time to turn off the heat.

d) Sprinkle your additives, cheese, salt, pepper and a tablespoon of chives in this case, and flip both sides from either end over the middle part. By flipping once more over the plate, you will get the folded side down below.

e) Serve hot.

32. Cream Cheese Omelet with Herbs

The standard cheese omelet has been slightly modified by this one as well. The delicate, delicious omelet and the creamy cheese go along beautifully. This cheesy omelet has nutritious ingredients. It is a timeless dish that is tasty at any time of day and is easy to prepare.

Serving Size: 2

Cooking Time: 6 Minutes

Ingredients:

- ¼ cup cilantro leaves, chopped
- 4 eggs
- 1 tbsp. butter
- 2 oz. softened cream cheese
- Salt and pepper to taste

Instructions:

a) Lightly whip the cream cheese with herb and seasonings in a bowl. First beat two eggs separately into a bowl. Remember that each serving has to be prepared separately.

b) Heat half of the butter in the skillet over medium heat. Let it get really hot and then pour the first two eggs in the pan. Within moments the eggs will start to coagulate. At this moment, use a spatula to push the omelet to one side of the pan so that the uncooked runs over to the cleared pan. You will have to do it one more time and then turn off the heat.

c) Take half of the cheese mixture and dab it onto the middle of the omelet. Spread it from one side to the other. Roll the omelet over and slide off onto a serving plate.

d) Serve hot.

33. Mushroom Quiche

Making a healthy quiche that is largely vegetarian couldn't be simpler. The crust on this quiche is amazing! Among other essential ingredients, it is loaded with sweetly sliced pork, milk, and eggs. Serve it with a simple salad for lunch or during breakfast or brunch.

Serving Size: 2

Cooking Time: 50 Minutes

Ingredients:

- ¾ tsp. salt
- ¼ tsp. freshly ground black pepper
- 1 cup sliced mushrooms
- 4 large eggs
- 2 medium shallots, thinly sliced and sautéed
- 6 oz. cubed pork
- 1 Precooked and cooled Savory Superfoods Pie Crust
- 1 cup coconut milk

Instructions:

a) Brown the pork in coconut oil and then add the mushrooms and shallots. Set aside once done.

b) Preheat the oven to 350^0F.

c) In a sizable bowl, combine eggs, milk, salt and pepper. Whisk until foamy. Add in about ¾ of the drained filling mixture, reserving the other ¼ to "top" the quiche. Pour egg mixture into the crust and place the remaining filling on top of the quiche.

d) Place quiche in the oven centered at the middle rack and bake undisturbed for 45 to 50 minutes.

e) Serve and enjoy.

34. A Hearty Australian Omelet

If you want a hearty breakfast that will satisfy both your taste senses and your appetite, try this dish. This breakfast meal features veggies, shrimp, and a tasty combination of spices. Enjoy!

Serving Size: 2

Cooking Time: 5 Minutes

Ingredients:

- ½ tomato sliced
- ¼ cup sliced mushrooms
- 6 medium shrimps, deveined and cleaned
- 3 eggs
- ¼ cup milk
- ½ clove crushed garlic
- 2 oz. cheddar cheese, shredded
- 1 ½ tsps. olive oil
- Salt and pepper to taste
- ½ tsps. curry powder
- 2 tbsps. green bell pepper, diced
- ½ onion, finely chopped

Instructions:

a) In a medium sized nonstick pan, add the garlic, onion, mushrooms with pepper and cook over medium heat, without oil, until opaque and tender.

b) In a bowl, mix together eggs, milk, curry powder, salt and black pepper. Now heat oil in a skillet. When hot, pour in the eggs and let it cook over medium heat for a few minutes, until just firm. Layer it up with cheese, tomato and onion mixture.

c) Fold one side of the eggs over the other and serve this scrumptious omelet warm.

35. Oats & Blueberry Cake

Enjoy the flavor of this unique Oats and Blueberry cake without worrying about your blood sugar levels or weight gain, thanks to the recipe's use of the best, most convenient, and family-friendly ingredients.

Serving Size: 3

Cooking Time: 30 Minutes

Ingredients:

- 1 tsp. ground vanilla bean
- ¼ tsp. salt
- 1 ½ cups almond milk
- 1 tsp. ground cinnamon
- ¾ cup blueberries
- 2 ½ cups old-fashioned rolled oats
- 1 beaten egg
- 1/3 cup raw honey
- 2 tbsps. coconut oil
- 1 tsp. baking powder

Instructions:

a) Combine oats and almond milk, cover and let soak in the fridge overnight.

b) Preheat the oven to 375°F. Stir the egg, honey, oil, vanilla, cinnamon, salt and baking powder into the oats until well combined. Mix in blueberries. Pour into an oiled pan.

c) Bake the oatmeal cake for 25 to 30 minutes. Let cool for 10 minutes. Loosen and remove from the pan.

d) Top with blueberries and raspberries and serve warm.

36. Dandelion Olives Quiche

For most people, Dandelion Olive Quiche is simply the finest and healthiest option. A great selection of standard, healthy ingredients are included in the recipe. Use the straightforward cooking directions to make the dish, and your family will be sure to like it.

Serving Size: 3

Cooking Time: 50 Minutes

Ingredients:

- ¾ cup sliced pitted olives
- 1 cup coconut milk
- ¼ tsp. freshly ground black pepper
- 1 Precooked and cooled Savory Superfoods Pie Crust
- 4 large eggs
- ¾ tsp. salt
- 2 cups chopped dandelion leaves

Instructions:

a) Preheat the oven to 350^0F.

b) In a sizable bowl, combine eggs, milk, salt and pepper. Whisk until foamy. Put dandelion and olives in the crust. Pour egg mixture over veggies in the crust.

c) Place quiche in the oven centered at the middle rack and bake undisturbed for 45 to 50 minutes.

d) Serve and enjoy.

37. Onions & Swiss Chard Quiche

The newest trends right now are Swiss chard quiches with onion and other vegetables. Chopped Swiss chard, a savory pie crust made from superfoods that have been precooked and chilled, eggs, and other ingredients are used in this straightforward and quick recipe for onion and Swiss chard quiche. When you want a dish that is both nutritious and stunning, this is ideal.

Serving Size: 3

Cooking Time: 50 Minutes

Ingredients:

- ¾ tsp. salt
- 4 large eggs
- ¼ tsp. freshly ground black pepper
- 1 Precooked and cooled Savory Superfoods Pie Crust
- 1 cup coconut milk
- 1 cup chopped onions
- 2 cups chopped Swiss Chard

Instructions:

a) Preheat the oven to 350^0F.

b) In a sizable bowl, combine eggs, milk, salt and pepper. Whisk until foamy. Put Swiss chard and onions in the crust. Pour egg mixture over veggies in the crust.

c) Place quiche in the oven centered at the middle rack and bake undisturbed for 45 to 50 minutes.

d) Serve and enjoy.

38. Eggs in Purgatory

You'll be thrilled to devour Eggs in Purgatory as a nutritious and expertly cooked dish for a relaxing weekend brunch or a memorable, unplanned midweek dinner. Although the thought of cooking eggs in tomatoes among other nutritious ingredients may seem weird, have you ever tried it? Get ready for that mouth-watering sensation.

Serving Size: 1

Cooking Time: 15 Minutes

Ingredients:

- 1 clove garlic, chopped.
- ¼ tsp. salt
- 1 tbsp. hot red pepper flakes and 1 tbsp. cilantro
- 1 tsp. olive oil or avocado oil
- 1 cup chopped tomatoes
- 2 large eggs

Instructions:

a) Heat 1 teaspoon of oil in a medium skillet over medium heat.

b) Add garlic, chopped tomatoes and red pepper flakes and cook, tossing approximately 15 minutes. Add eggs and cook until eggs are done. Sprinkle it with salt and cilantro.

c) Serve and enjoy.

39. Tomato Quiche

This delicious quiche with tomatoes is suitable for breakfast, a light meal, or perhaps the evening. This quiche will be wonderful for every meal of the day because of its ideal blend of ingredients, which also includes eggs, coconut milk, and pork.

Serving Size: 3

Cooking Time: 50 Minutes

Ingredients:

- ¼ cup. arugula
- 1 cup coconut milk
- ¼ tsp. freshly ground black pepper
- 1 Precooked and cooled Savory Superfoods Pie Crust
- 6 oz. cubed pork
- 2 medium shallots, thinly sliced and sautéed
- ¾ tsp. salt
- 4 large eggs
- 1 cup sliced tomatoes

Instructions:

a) Brown the pork and shallots in the coconut oil. Set aside once done.

b) Preheat the oven to 350^{0}F.

c) In a sizable bowl, combine eggs, milk, salt and pepper. Whisk until foamy. Add in about ¾ of the drained filling mixture and tomatoes, reserving the other ¼ to "top" the quiche. Pour egg mixture into the crust and place remaining filling on top of the quiche.

d) Place quiche in the oven centered at the middle rack and bake undisturbed for 45 to 50 minutes. Sprinkle with arugula.

e) Serve and enjoy.

40. Frittata with Asparagus and Tomato

With a set of carefully picked ingredients including asparagus, eggs, and tomatoes among other additive ingredients, this Italian-style frittata with asparagus and tomatoes is somewhat crispier and sweeter and packs a flavor punch through the middle.

Serving Size: 1

Cooking Time: 5 Minutes

Ingredients:

- 1 tsp. olive oil or avocado oil
- ½ cup sliced tomatoes
- 2 large eggs
- ¼ tsp. ground black pepper
- 1 cup asparagus
- ¼ tsp. salt

Instructions:

a) Whisk 2 large eggs in a sizable bowl. Season with salt and ground black pepper and set aside.

b) Heat 1 teaspoon of oil in a medium skillet over medium heat.

c) Add asparagus and cook, tossing approximately 5 minutes. Add tomatoes and eggs and cook, stirring occasionally, until just set, about 1 minute.

d) Sprinkle with dill before serving.

41. Prosciutto Eggs

Easy to prepare ahead of time, your friends will enjoy these prosciutto baked eggs. You can be sure that your family will appreciate these delectable times when they are baked in prosciutto with eggs and other essential ingredients prepared to perfection.

Serving Size: 2

Cooking Time: 15 Minutes

Ingredients:

- ½ lemon, zested and juiced
- 1 pinch ground black pepper
- 4 eggs
- 1 tbsp. extra-virgin olive oil
- 1 tbsp olive oil
- 1 tsp distilled white vinegar
- 1 pinch salt
- ¼ tsp. ground black pepper
- 2 oz. minced prosciutto
- 1 bunch fresh asparagus, trimmed

Instructions:

a) Set your oven to 425^0F before doing anything else.

b) Get a casserole dish and enter into it your asparagus and coat the veggies with some olive oil.

c) Stir fry your prosciutto and some black pepper for 5 minutes in 1 tablespoon of olive oil.

d) Layer the meat over the asparagus. Bake for 10 minutes.

e) Then toss the contents and bake for 6 more minutes.

f) Boil 3 inches of water and add in some salt and your vinegar.

g) Then break an egg in the water. Continue for all eggs. Let the eggs poach for 6 minutes. Then remove them from the water.

h) Now plate your asparagus and coat them with a bit of lemon juice then topped with an egg. Then some zest of lemon and finally a bit of pepper.

i) Enjoy.

42. Egg Cooker Whoopie Pie

Take a bite of something delicious from your egg cooker. This nostalgic pie is a simple classic made with soft, moist, and sweet ingredients like cake mix, icing made with vanilla, and eggs, among others. A wonderful opportunity for the youngsters.

Serving Size: 2

Cooking Time: 3 Minutes

Ingredients:

- 1 tsp. vegetable oil
- 1 2/3 cups Devil's food cake mix
- 1 egg
- 12 oz. whipped vanilla frosting
- ½ cup sour cream

Instructions:

a) Lightly grease your Microwave Egg Cooker with oil.

b) Combine your egg, cake mix, and sour and whisk until fully blended.

c) Evenly divide your batter into 4 greased egg cooker cups and all to cook on high in the microwave until the center becomes firm for about 2½ minutes.

d) Carefully drop your mini cakes out of the egg cooker and allow to cool completely. Generously frost the flat side of 2 of the cakes, cover with two other mini cakes to create your delicious whoopie pies.

e) Serve and enjoy.

43. Buttery Eggs

Should milk be added to scrambled eggs? No, however, they do help the food stay moist and tasty longer. Try it out now, please. The time is right to break from the conventional method of cracking eggs into a hot skillet and stirring them until they are fully cooked, which results in hard eggs with distinct white and yolk striations. The buttery eggs are delicious!

Serving Size: 3

Cooking Time: 6 Minutes

Ingredients:

- Salt and pepper to taste
- 1/8 tsp. ground white pepper
- 6 eggs
- 2 tbsps. all-purpose flour
- 2 cups milk
- 2 tbsps. butter

Instructions:

a) Get a big saucepan and fill it with water. Add your eggs to the water and bring it to a rolling boil. Once boiling for about a minute then remove the pan from the heat and place a lid on it. Let it stand for about 13 minutes.

b) After 13 minutes, take out the eggs, remove the shells, and dice them.

c) Now drain the saucepan of its water and melt some butter in it. Once the butter is melted add some flour and heat it until a ball-like shape begins to form. Then add in your milk and lightly stir until the sauce begins to boil.

d) While boiling add in: salt, white pepper, chopped eggs, and black pepper. Heat everything up then remove it all from the heat.

e) Enjoy with your favorite toasted bread.

44. Pepperoni Omelet

It's similar to a pizza-filled omelet that children can easily adore.

Serving Size: 2

Cooking Time: 5 Minutes

Ingredients:

- 2 tbsps. chopped green onions
- 2 eggs
- ⅛ tsp. salt
- 1/8 cup pepperoni
- 2 tbsps. milk

Instructions:

a) Combine the milk, salt and eggs in your Ceramic Egg Cooker.

b) Cover, rest your finger on top of the small hole in the lid and shake well to combine. Stir in your pepperoni and cheese.

c) Set to cook in the microwave, covered, for about a minute on high. Remove and stir, then return to cook until fully cooked through, stirring in 20-second intervals.

d) Serve, and enjoy.

45. Bacon Omelet

Like anything else, this omelet is better when it is prepared with bacon. For the greatest tastes in this fluffy omelet, combine green onions, milk, bacon pieces, and eggs through a proper set of instructions. This bacon omelet dish offers a mouthful of cheesy goodness, crispy bacon, and a selection of healthy ingredients.

Serving Size: 2

Cooking Time: 10 Minutes

Ingredients:

- 2 tbsps. green onions, chopped
- 1 tbsp. cheddar cheese
- 2 eggs
- 4 bacon strips, crispy and chopped
- 2 tbsps. milk
- ⅛ tsp. salt

Instructions:

a) Combine eggs, milk and salt in your Ceramic Egg Cooker.

b) Cover, rest your finger on top of the small hole in the lid and shake well to combine. Stir in your chopped bacon and cheese.

c) Set to cook in the microwave, covered, for about a minute on high. Remove and stir, then return to cook until fully cooked through, stirring in 20-second intervals.

d) Serve, and enjoy.

46. Spicy Deviled Eggs

Smoked paprika's taste complements this dish quite well. The traditional meals get a spicy touch from Spicy Deviled Eggs. The splash of yogurt and mustard provide a wonderful taste that you won't be able to resist! A must-have for any celebration or event.

Serving Size: 10

Cooking Time: 8 Minutes

Ingredients:

- 2 tbsps. butter
- ¼ tsp. salt and pepper
- 1 tbsp. Dijon mustard
- 5 eggs
- 1 tsp smoked paprika
- ½ tsp. garlic powder
- 2 chives, chopped
- ½ cup yogurt

Instructions:

a) Hard boil the eggs for 8 minutes.

b) Add to a cold wash.

c) Remove the egg shells.

d) Cut the eggs in half.

e) Take the egg yolks in a bowl and mash using a fork.

f) Add the yogurt and mix well.

g) Add the smoked paprika, butter, Dijon mustard, garlic powder and mix.

h) Use a spoon and add in the middle of each egg shell.

i) Sprinkle some paprika on top. Add chives on top.

47. Macaroni and Eggs

This Macaroni and Eggs meal is bursting with a hearty and delicious taste and ready in just a few minutes. This macaroni meal will satisfy everyone because it is made with your favorite macaroni, butter, and eggs, among other ingredients. Wonderful lunch on a workday.

Serving Size: 2

Cooking Time: 6 Minutes

Ingredients:

- 4 large eggs, lightly beaten
- 1 ½ cups elbow macaroni
- ¼ tsp. paprika
- Salt and ground black pepper to taste
- 1 tbsp. butter

Instructions:

a) Boil macaroni in salt and water for 9 minutes until al dente.

b) Get a frying pan and melt some butter in it. Then add in your pasta to the melted butter along with some: pepper, paprika, and salt.

c) Add eggs to the pasta and do not stir anything for 2 minutes. Then for 6 minutes continue cooking the eggs but now you can stir. Turn off the heat.

d) Place a lid on the pan and let the eggs continue to cook without heat.

e) Serve and enjoy.

48. Red Beet Deviled Eggs

This recipe for deviled eggs is special since it calls for a creamy, gooey egg combination in addition to other essential ingredients. Lovely beet-pickled deviled eggs are made simply and deliciously. It is a filling dish for a large group.

Serving Size: 6

Cooking Time: 3 Hours

Ingredients:

- 1 red beet, halved
- 2 tbsps. cilantro, chopped
- 1 tsp. anchovy paste
- 1 tbsp. sugar
- ½ cup mayo
- 1 jalapeno, sliced
- 12 eggs
- ¼ tsp. salt and pepper
- 1 cup apple cider vinegar

Instructions:

a) Remove the eggs' shells after hard boiling them.

b) In a pot, combine the sugar, apple cider vinegar, salt, and 3 cups of water.

c) Add the red beet and bring it to boil.

d) Take off the heat. Let it cool down.

e) Add the boiled eggs and leave for 3 hours.

f) Cut the eggs in half.

g) Add the egg yolks in a bowl.

h) Mix in the mayo, anchovy paste, salt, pepper, cilantro, and 1 tablespoon of vinegar.

i) Mix well. Pipe into the egg whites.

j) Add the jalapeno on top.

49. Avocado Herb Deviled Eggs

The Avocado Herb Deviled Eggs taste so good and are also really attractive. They serve as the best meal with a proper combination of ingredients for a healthier afternoon or a fresh start for the day.

Serving Size: 10

Cooking Time: 8 Minutes

Ingredients:

- 1 tsp. garlic powder
- 1 tbsp. butter
- 5 eggs
- 1/3 cup ripe avocado, cubed
- 1 tbsp. coriander, chopped
- ¼ tsp. salt and pepper
- 1/3 cup yogurt
- 1 tbsp. butter

Instructions:

a) Hard boil the eggs for 8 minutes.

b) Remove the shells and cut them in half.

c) In a bowl, combine the egg yolk with avocado cubes.

d) Mash using a fork. Add the butter and yogurt.

e) Mix well. Add garlic, salt, and pepper. Mix well.

f) Spoon out the mixture and add in the middle of each egg white.

g) Top with coriander. Serve.

50. Eggs in Bread

Eggs and butter are used to add a lovely taste to this pillowy soft and mouth-watering eggs in Bread dish. A great addition to butter and jam for breakfast! Enjoy!

Serving Size: 1

Cooking Time: 4 Minutes

Ingredients:

- 1 egg
- ½ tbsp. butter
- 1 slice white bread

Instructions:

a) Coat your bread with butter on each of its sides. Then cut-out a circle in the middle of it.

b) Whisk your egg in a small bowl. Set it aside.

c) Get a skillet hot and for 1 minute, fry each side of the bread. Pour the egg into the hole and cook for 3 more minutes.

d) Enjoy.

51. Soy Sriracha Deviled Eggs

You should try making deviled eggs with soy sauce and sriracha. Don't miss the chance to prepare this incredible appetizer if you haven't tried the dish before.

Serving Size: 8

Cooking Time: 3 Minutes

Ingredients:

- ½ cup yogurt
- ½ tsp. sriracha
- 1 cup rice vinegar
- 1 tsp. smoked paprika
- 2 tbsps. chives
- 4 eggs
- ¼ tsp. salt and pepper
- 2 tbsps. tomato sauce
- 1 cup mirin
- 1 cup soy sauce

Instructions:

a) In a large bowl, combine the mirin, soy sauce, sriracha and rice vinegar. Mix and set aside.

b) In a pot, hard boil the eggs.

c) Remove the egg shells.

d) Now dip them in the mirin mix for 24 hours.

e) Cut the eggs in half. Take out the yolks.

f) Add them to a bowl. Mash them finely.

g) Mix in the smoked paprika, salt, pepper, tomato sauce, and yogurt and then make a smooth mix. Scoop into the egg shells.

h) Serve with chives and more tomato sauce on top.

52. Tomato, Basil Mozzarella Quiche

Use your egg cooker to prepare this delectable weekend brunch menu quickly. Breakfast, a light lunch, or even evening would be appropriate times to serve this tomato, basil, and mozzarella quiche. This quiche will be great for every meal of the day with its handmade flavors and ingredients, including egg and luscious plum tomatoes.

Serving Size: 1

Cooking Time: 20 Minutes

Ingredients:

- 4 basil leaves, fresh and finely chopped
- 1 tsp. salt and pepper each, to taste
- 1 tsp. olive oil
- 2 eggs
- 1 plum tomato, sliced
- 1 mini pie crust, frozen
- 3 tbsps. milk
- ¾ cup, grated mozzarella cheese

Instructions:

a) Set your oven to preheat to 400^0F. Press your mini crusts into your egg cooker. Prick the edges of your dough.

b) Top your baked crust with your cheese, basil, and tomato evenly.

c) Combine your remaining ingredients in a medium bowl and whisk to combine then pour on top in your crust. Set to bake until fully set for about 20 minutes.

d) Cool, serve and enjoy!

Conclusion

The egg is one of several ingredients that are important in meals. It can be used as a major meal, an accouterment to other foods, or an ingredient in other foods. Whether you already have them prepared in the kitchen or are intending to get them from the market, including eggs in your meals or dishes offers excellent nutrients and unrivaled flavor.

The egg is regarded as a major component in culinary preparation because of its versatility, which gives dishes moisture, texture, and flavor. When prepared and utilized appropriately, it may also emulsify and aerate your meal along with its constituent ingredients. Eggs are also healthy. Therefore, the mix of recipes in this book creates a good approach to use eggs in your meals for a terrific, delicious, nutritious, and healthy experience. With a large selection of family-friendly, healthier dishes, this egg cookbook provides different novel methods for cooking eggs. Simply said, it's a simpler method that enables egg lovers to delight in enticing, original dishes right from their own kitchens.

Try out these recipes and have a wholesome experience of the perfect flavors from eggs alongside other important ingredients.

Biography

Samantha Rich is a dynamic and creative writer who has a passion for cooking and writing recipes. Born and raised in the United States, she has always had a love for food and the art of cooking. From a young age, Samantha was always eager to try new recipes and experiment with flavors, and her family encouraged her creativity in the kitchen.

Samantha's love for cooking and writing only grew as she got older, and she eventually pursued a degree in culinary arts and writing. She honed her skills in the kitchen, and her writing talent soon became apparent. She began publishing her recipes in local newspapers and food blogs, and her writing quickly caught the attention of others in the culinary world.

In her early twenties, Samantha decided to take her passion to the next level by writing a cookbook. Her first cookbook was a success, and she quickly gained Over the next few years, she continued to write more cookbooks, each one showcasing her unique voice and culinary creativity.

Today, Samantha Rich is a well-respected and beloved author in the cooking and writing community. Her cookbooks are enjoyed by home cooks and professional chefs alike, and she has become known for her ability to create recipes that are both delicious and accessible. Whether she's writing about classic comfort food or innovative new dishes, Samantha's writing is always infused with her love for cooking and her passion for sharing that love with others.

When she's not in the kitchen or writing, Samantha enjoys spending time with her family and friends, trying new restaurants, and exploring new recipes from around the world. She continues to be a sought-after speaker and presenter, and her fans are always eager to see what she'll come up with next.

Afterword's

Wow, what an incredible experience this has been. I couldn't have done it without your support and participation. As an author, I can only write the words, but it's up to the reader to bring them to life. And you did exactly that. You purchased this book, dedicated your time to reading it, and reached the end with me. I am deeply humbled.

While you've already done so much, I have one more request. I value feedback from my readers and would love to hear your thoughts on the book. I would be grateful if you could leave a review on Amazon. Not only will I see it, but it will also give others the opportunity to discover the book as well. The book community is a special one, and by sharing your thoughts, you are contributing to its growth and success.

Thank you for being so awesome.

Samantha Rich

Printed in Great Britain
by Amazon

5d398d06-e631-45db-bb36-5f1d3a9bcaf7R01